# If a
# Picture
**Paints a Thousand Words**

# If a Picture Paints a Thousand Words

### Give Your Child the Right Foundation for a Biblical Worldview

Joseph Stephen

Joseph Stephen
If a Picture Paints a Thousand Words
© 2009, 2014 by Joseph Stephen. All rights reserved.

ISBN: 978-0-9924875-1-5

All rights reserved. No part of this book may be reproduced without written permission from the publisher or copyright holder, except in the case of brief quotations embodied in critical articles and reviews. No part of this book may be transmitted in any form or by any means—electronic, mechanical, photocopy, recording, or other—without prior written permission from the publisher or copyright holder.

All Scriptures are taken from The *King James Version* of the Holy Bible.

I dedicate this book to our cherished children, Caleb, Gideon, Micah, Hannah, Esther (with the Lord), Amos, Moses, Noah and Abigail, whom God has so graciously entrusted to our care. May you live out the words of Joshua that I have shared with you so often:

Joshua 22:5 But take diligent heed ... to love the Lord your God, and to walk in all his ways, and to keep his commandments, and to cleave unto him, and to serve him with all your heart and with all your soul.

# Contents

| | |
|---|---|
| Acknowledgments | ix |
| Foreword | xiii |
| Introduction | xv |
| 1. Dualism and Distortion in Children's Books | 1 |
| 2. A Biblical Worldview | 19 |
| 3. God's Primary Means of Communication | 23 |
| 4. Pictures in Scripture | 27 |
| 5. Images Lead to Destruction | 35 |
| 6. Thinking Like a Child | 45 |
| 7. Why Read? | 51 |
| 8. Excuses | 55 |
| Conclusion | 59 |

# Acknowledgments

THIS BOOK IS a direct result of my precious bride Florence's God given gift of discernment. Florence has directed my attention to many of the major issues in life for which I now hold a personal conviction. Without her eyes, my world would be very dark; without her love, it would be very cold; and without her reproof I would not be able to see the many areas of my life needing correction. I thank God for giving me such a necessary and suitable companion. I would like to thank Florence for pointing out the classic illustrations and scenarios described in these pages. I am extremely grateful for the many hours Florence spent finding the appropriate illustrations and proofreading the manuscript, simultaneously continuing to be a wife, mother, home keeper, home educator and friend.

I thank my children who have made me aware of so many areas of life needing to come under the lordship of Christ as they reflect various aspects of my own character.

I thank Pastor Greg McPherson for his keen eye in helping to proofread the manuscript and find areas needing further clarification or correction.

Finally I thank my Lord Jesus Christ without whom there would be no purpose or meaning to life. The Lord not only gives eternal life, He defines the very reason for our existence on earth since it is He who created us, sustains us and gives purpose to our being here. My desire in writing this book is simply to encourage all readers to give God the glory due His name (Ps. 29:2) through total surrender to His will and submission to His Lordship in every area of life, including how we teach our children.

**Acknowledgments**   xi

# Foreword

JOSEPH, I HAVE just finished reading your book. I agree with it wholeheartedly. Yes we must get back to the Bible, and if using pictures then use ones that are uplifting and pointing towards the Lord Jesus Christ, not drawing us and our loved ones away from our Lord and Saviour. I especially like the part about "But children need these pictures," otherwise they get bored. This is the problem today. We adults are putting thoughts into our children's and young peoples' heads by suggesting such things. So the children, not wanting to disappoint us, respond with the catch-cry, "I'm bored."

I would encourage you to read this book and to carefully consider what Joseph has written. As parents, grandparents and pastors, consider what appetite you are creating in the heart of the child you are giving that book to. Is it going to create a heart that seeks after God, or is it going to draw that child away from a life of serving the Lord Jesus Christ?

—Greg McPherson
Pastor of Old Paths Bible Church
Strathalbyn, South Australia.

# Introduction

SOME WEEKS AGO, my eldest son came to me and described how Saul of Tarsus fell off his horse when the Lord Jesus met him on the road to Damascus (Acts 9:3). I asked him where he heard that. His reply was simple: "I saw it in a book." He ran and fetched the book and began describing the horse, the men standing around, and Saul on the ground. I told him this was just a book and that the Bible did not say anything about Saul falling off his horse, only that he fell to the ground. He was indignant as if to imply, "You gave me this book and it's not true? What else isn't true?" Actually we didn't give him the book, but it was one of many gifts from a well-meaning and very dear family friend whose genuine desire is to help us raise godly children by providing them with Bible stories. Our children read lots of books. I wondered what other distortions were going to be raised in conversation as we discussed Bible stories. This example may make you laugh, but it raises a very fundamental issue that I hope to address in these pages.

Ever since we had children, my wife has carefully scrutinized their books, toys, furniture, clothes, and everything else that can have children's cartoons printed on them. We want to ensure that they meet a strict standard. The children knew from very young how to discern folly, and they came to her to white-out or correct the pictures. This instance, however, started me on a journey to discover just exactly what God thinks about images as a means to communicating truth. Images may on the surface seem harmless at first, but when you realize just how many of our children's books contain unbiblical facts, untenable assertions, false assumptions, dubious interpretations and outright contradictions, it's no wonder their scriptural foundations are undermined.

## Chapter 1

# Dualism and Distortion in Children's Books

**H**AVE YOU EVER read a story to a child and shown him or her pictures of the unfolding drama? Have you ever asked a child what they remember about a story? Have you ever been interrupted by your child as you were reading and asked an insignificant or irrelevant question having to do with a drawing or photograph? If so, this is probably the point where you realize your child's attention was probably not with you at all, but rather on analysing something totally irrelevant to the story. It is usually true that a child's memory is more indelibly imprinted with pictures rather than words. Even now, my wife, who came from a Catholic background before she was gloriously saved through reading the Scriptures alone, says that whenever she thinks of the Lord Jesus, she sees the erroneous Roman Catholic depictions of Him with long blond hair, blue eyes, fair skin, skinny build and no muscles. In short, a Jesus who is rather effeminate and weak. This simple contradiction against what the Bible says about the Lord Jesus has far reaching ramifications, as Christian boys especially mistakenly emulate this depiction rather than true manliness consistent with God's design and revealed Word.

As a small child, my wife was afraid to discard inanimate objects portrayed in books with human faces. She thought that throwing away old shoes, hair brushes and other possessions was going to hurt their feelings. While this might instill a good character trait of caring for one's possessions, it does so by using a wrong motive. Rather than valuing inanimate possessions for what they cost their parents, children identify with the human faces and values such possessions for their human-like status.

A valuable experiment is to take a children's book, cover the words, and tell the story from the pictures. Then cover the pictures and read the written text. You will be shocked to observe the difference. This difference is called *dualism,* and it is the effect of telling two different stories at the same time, one through pictures and one through words. Following stories through pictures gives a child the impression they are learning something, but in fact they are remembering a conflicting record. This becomes even more apparent with very young children who can't yet read and rely solely on the pictures to tell the story.

A storybook on creation, for example, showed a picture of the sun for day one as it described how God created light. But this is not a correct depiction. The Bible says that the sun was created on the fourth day (Gen.1:3-5; 16-19). When a child recalls the story, more often than not they will associate light with the sun rather than with God, who called light out of nothing. Another classic example is the story of Noah's ark, where the ark is depicted as a construction with many windows with cute giraffes looking out and gentle rain falling upon the ground. In truth, the ark according to Scripture had a single door and window (Gen. 6:16). According to the Scripture, the windows of heaven and the fountains of the deep were broken up, creating a tumultuous storm of unprecedented proportions (Gen. 7:11). There were no giraffes looking out the window at the gentle drizzle since the single window of the ark was set a cubit from the top, making it too high for the animals to look out (Gen. 6:16). Pictures showing animals on the deck, sticking out of windows and playing on the tops of doors in a calm sea do not begin to demonstrate the true catastrophic event.

God also explicitly distinguishes between clean and unclean animals going into the ark. Noah was commanded to take seven, not two of every clean beast. He was also commanded to take seven of every fowl of the air (Gen. 7:2-3, 8). Seven is God's perfect number and is significant, as are many numbers in the Bible. Illustrating the clean animals by twos contradicts God's Word and removes His own explicit distinction of clean and unclean, holy and unholy (Lev. 10:10, 11:47, 11:2-30).

The serpent speaking to Eve in the Garden of Eden is often depicted as a snake, and the forbidden

The picture shows animals on the deck of a tiny overcrowded houseboat on a calm sea. The real ark was gigantic, had three decks, one window and one door. Animals would not have been on the deck during the tumult nor after it. The animals only left the ark on God's command. Note that there should be seven of each clean animal pictured (such as sheep) rather than only two.

fruit is usually assumed to be an apple. Yet neither is true. It wasn't until punishment was pronounced that the serpent crawled on its belly (Gen. 3:14). Meanwhile, we are not told what the fruit of the knowledge of good and evil was.

Why are these sorts of misrepresentations dangerous? There is a phenomenon known as subliminal suggestion. Think of the Coca-Cola ad flashed on the screen for a single frame every

# 6  If a Picture Paints a Thousand Words

The picture shows the serpent as a snake and the forbidden fruit an apple. Both are untrue.

few minutes during a movie. You don't even know you're seeing the ad, but subconsciously it is registering and plays out its effects when you least expect. The next time you're faced with the decision about what to drink at the local café, guess what comes to mind? What pictures effectively do is undermine words to the point that at a later date, recollection of the story will weigh heavily on the mental picture rather than the written word. This is not a problem if the pictures or photographs are one hundred percent accurate. But if they tell a totally different story, then it is that subliminal story that will be subconsciously believed.

Another example my wife came across more recently was a clock in the shape of a school house with the caption of Proverbs 22:6 "Train up a child in the way he should go and when

## Dualism and Distortion in Children's Books 7

he is old he will not depart." Instantly, one associates the training of children with school. Even a cursory study of Proverbs teaches that the training being referred to in this verse, and indeed the entire Bible, is parental training, not public education. But this schoolhouse-shaped clock undermines the Scriptures and leaves the impression that school and not the home is the method of child training implied by the Bible (Prov. 1:8; 2:1; 3:1, 12; 4:1,10-11, 20; 5:1; 6:20; 7:1; 13:1; 23:22, 26). Incorrect pictures communicate false assumptions which lead to false conclusions.

Let us consider another seemingly harmless phenomenon, the children's book containing cute animals dressed in clothing and given the characteristics of humans. This sort of depiction is now so prevalent I'm going to find it hard to make my point unless my reader is willing to take the Scriptures as the sole authority in all matters. What do such pictures teach? They teach that animals are equal to humans! This is exactly what the religion of humanism teaches in its doctrine of evolution. Why do we wear clothes? We wear clothes to cover our nakedness because we have knowledge of sin through Adam. Animals firstly were not created equal to man (Gen. 1:26-28, 9:2; 1 Cor. 15:39-41) or else Eve wouldn't have been created (Gen. 2:20-24), and secondly animals have no knowledge of sin nor do they share the character traits of humans, not being created in the image of God (Gen. 1:27). Birds are not endowed with understanding or wisdom as we give the owl credit (Job 39:13-17). The mule and horse have no understanding (Ps. 32:9). Bears are not cute, they do not love,

**This picture shows a rabbit dressed in a coat, sitting upright holding and eating radishes with hand-like paws. Man was created in the image of God, so to make an animal act like man is to equate an animal to the image of God! We wear clothing to cover our nakedness because of our consciousness of sin, which animals do not possess.**

they do not care about people, and they cannot comfort anyone. In truth, they are savage (Hosea 13:8, Prov. 17:12, 2 Kings 2:24).

Why then do we comfort our children with such falsehood? You may say that surely children know in real life that animals don't wear clothes, so why should they think that they are created equal to humans? The proof is in the evidence. Animals have been exalted to above human status to the point that numerous people grow up loving animals more than they love children! Equating animals to humans is blasphemy because it implies they were created in God's image. This was brought home very strongly when a recent news article on cruelty to a baby koala drew a flurry of public comment, while the tragic death of a young child drew almost none. We now have animal rights organizations and many in our society who worship animals, expending great resources to save the whales, while millions of unborn babies are murdered through abortion and abortifacient contraceptives, without a second thought. (Abortifacient contraceptives include the morning-after pill, the contraceptive pill, the IUD, Norplant and Depo-Provera.)

Children's books are also full of pictures of the sun or moon with faces. Where did this practice come from, and is it really harmless? The ancients worshiped the host of heaven, the sun god, the moon god, and myriads of other gods. That face on the sun or moon in your children's book is not harmless because, once again, this attributes characteristics and status to celestial bodies not granted them by the true God of the Bible (Deut. 4:19, 17:3; 2 Kings 17:16, 21:3, 23:4-5; Jer. 8:2; etc.). Even the hosts of heaven, including all other worldly bodies, worship the true God (Neh. 9:6).

The last and most poisonous example of how images corrupt the truth is the standard representation of the Lord Himself—His birth,

On the fourth day God put the sun, the moon, and the stars in the sky. So there was evening, and there was morning.

**The picture shows faces on the sun and moon (celestial pagan worship) and irreverently and erroneously portrays the Invisible and Almighty God.**

## Dualism and Distortion in Children's Books 11

life and death. The distortion begins with the birth of the Lord Jesus and continues right through His earthly life. Many traditional children's illustrations distort, deny or deduce things from the Bible that the Bible does not support. Scripture says nothing, for example, about the number of wise men who did not come to the manger but came to the house when the Lord was older (Matt. 2:11).

Angels in Scripture are male without exception and yet in children's books they are almost always portrayed as female—or males with long

The picture shows the three wise men at the stable to see the new born king. The Bible says shepherds and not wise men went to the birthplace; the wise men (the Bible does not mention how many) went to the house when the Lord was older.

hair. This is so prevalent it is commonplace to call little girls little angels. Even if this term is used only to describe the behavior of little girls, this is still wrong because we are all born with a sin nature (Rom. 5:12).

As already noted earlier, the weak and effeminate images of the Mighty God (Isa. 9:6) cast Him in a light that becomes the

**Picture shows angels as girls when scripture always describes them as men.**

foundational point of identification for the rest of many children's lives. In fact, the Lord Jesus was a carpenter (Mark 6:3), ruddy and rugged. Since Isaiah 53:2 describes Him as having no beauty, we can assume He was plain. The Lord was not readily recognizable from other men, and this is why it was necessary for God the Father to identify Him to John the Baptist

(John 1:33-34) and also why Judas betrayed Him with a kiss to identify Him to the mob (Luke 22:47-48).

On one occasion He turned the tables in the temple and used a whip to drive out those who were buying and selling, demonstrating righteous anger (John 2:13-16). This is not something a weak or effeminate man could or would do. He also demonstrated immense fortitude enduring the scourging and mockery of His trial, bore His own cross at least part of the way to Golgotha to be crucified (John 19:17, Luke 23:26), did not surrender in weakness but chose to lay His own life down (John 10:18), and had the power to take it up again. The Lord Jesus most certainly didn't have long hair, or Paul would have condemned his Lord and Saviour in 1 Corinthians 11:14 where the apostle describes long hair on a man as shameful.

Most depictions of the Lord Jesus on the cross are generally illustrated with His body completely intact and tiny blood marks around the nails in His palms. Showing the Lord as bloodless and unmarred is incorrigible, because it thoroughly destroys the impact and the truth of what actually happened at the original scene. The Lord of Glory had his appearance disfigured to the point He was unrecognizable (Isa. 52:14). He was scourged (John 19:1), had a crown of thorns pushed into His head (John 19:2), and was continually smitten by the soldiers (John 19:3). The Lord Jesus was then humiliated by being spat upon, having His beard plucked off (Isa. 50:6; Matt. 27:30) and being crucified without His garments (John 19:23-24). Finally a spear was driven into His side, after which blood and water flowed out (John 19:34).

No picture fit to look upon could adequately portray the gruesome horror of the actual scene at Calvary. Any attempt to illustrate these events would detract from the reality of its truth and would defile the mind to lay eyes on.

We must realize that the Father of Lies (John 8:44) has his own agenda to poison the minds of our little ones. Even Satan is portrayed as an impish devil with horns, when in reality he

This picture shows the body of the Lord Jesus as bloodless and intact, whereas the Scripture describes Him as marred beyond recognition. The fair and skinny Jesus in a white loin cloth and with long hair is fanciful.

is transformed into an angel of light (2 Cor. 11:14-15) and is often unrecognized as he roams the earth like a roaring lion seeking whom he may devour (1 Pet. 5:8).

As Isaiah 28:9-10 describes, children's learning is line upon line, precept upon precept, here a little, there a little. Each so-called "harmless" error is built upon another "harmless" error until the entire monolith of their learning is faulty from the ground up.

> Whom shall he teach knowledge? and whom shall he make to understand doctrine? them that are weaned from the milk, and drawn from the breasts. For precept must be upon precept, precept upon precept; line upon line, line upon line; here a little, and there a little.
> —Isaiah 28:9-10

It might not be so bad if pictures such as these were rare occurrences where a child could be corrected in their thinking by an alert adult who knows the truth. Unfortunately, however, children's books are saturated with such dualism and distortion. The worst part is that adults assume this is harmless—even necessary and good. What we are doing is weaving truth and falsity into a fabric forming the basis for our children's understanding of life. We don't even point out the lies as we go, and indeed we can't because they are too numerous. Nevertheless, we are warned that lies are linked directly to the searing of one's conscience as with a hot iron (1 Tim. 4:2), which is why we are exhorted to put away lying and speak the truth one to another as we are members of one another (Eph. 4:25). Why should we have a different rule for children? Why should we engage in a practice leading to the searing of children's consciences?

Dualism worked out in its fullest form leads to adults leading dual lives, one secular and one sacred. Worse still, we don't even realise that we're doing it. It leads to people communicating one thing through their words and another through their lives. Since such pictures are the steady diet of our youngest children, their very foundation of Biblical truth is destroyed even before it is finished being laid. In Psalm eleven, verse three, David asked, "If the foundations be destroyed, what can the righteous do?" A house built on such a foundation will not stand the test of storms of opposition, and we are told in Luke 6:49 that the ruin of that house will be great.

The end result of this dualism is immunization against the truth as Bible stories are relegated to the status of fables, unbelievable and powerless to impact the heart and soul. I've actually heard children from a seemingly strong Christian family describing Bible stories as just that—fables. I've also heard a father indignantly defend his son's long hair, saying that if it was good enough for Jesus to have long hair, then it was good enough for his son. His perception was a direct result of the classic imagery we have presented.

*Chapter 2*

# A Biblical Worldview

A WORLDVIEW IS a lens through which we see life. A Biblical worldview uses the lens of the Scriptures to see and evaluate everything, whereas in a Humanistic worldview human reasoning is the lens through which one sees reality. Now human reasoning is not always wrong, but it is always wrong when it is derived from a foundation leaving God out of the equation. And it is wrong when it contradicts clear precepts, established Biblical patterns or principles.

Secular humanism is a religion because it is the worship of the self. It is the denial of a supreme God and of accountability to Him, and it is governed by self interest or a life centered on human interests. A humanistic philosophy rejects God and instead emphasizes self-realization through reason. Without God, humanism claims we are basically randomly colliding atoms, and beyond the physical material of which we are composed, nothing else exists.

Humanism has its preachers, its gospel and its believers. Christians have allowed the preachers of humanism into their pulpits, schools and homes. This is not an extreme view because once we stop seeing every aspect of life from a Biblical worldview, and once we employ the methods and theories of humanism to life's problems, we become humanistic in our thinking rather than Christian. Many give lip service saying they hold the Bible as the sole authority on all matters of life. But then they adopt the patterns and practises of the humanists in many areas of life, because they do not discern the conflict between the two worldviews.

The idea that humans and animals are equal and that we should have a higher regard for the survival of animals than we do of human babies stems from the humanistic theory of evolution. After all, it's just the survival of the fittest. When we teach our children that people are equal to animals, we deny the Biblical truth that we were created in the image of God to have dominion over all the animals (Gen. 1:27-28; Ps. 8:5-8). Also, the idea that humans and animals are equal leads to an unhealthy love of animals by children who prefer the company of a puppy to that of a sibling.

Does God instruct us in the Scriptures as to how we should teach His Word to our children? Does it speak to the danger of using visual images? Does the Bible itself ever use pictures? Let us lay aside the baggage of our own upbringing and take the Sola Scriptura or "Scripture alone" challenge.

*Chapter 3*

# God's Primary Means of Communication

ROMANS 10:17 TEACHES US that faith comes by hearing the Word of God. God communicated directly to man via spoken word (Gen. 1:28-29, 2:16-17, 3:8-9; Exod. 3:4-6; Jer. 22:2; Amos 7:16; John 17:1 4; Acts 9:1-6; and Hebrews 2:1-2), via the written word on tablets of stone (Exod. 31:18), on the wall (Dan. 5:5), and even on the ground (John 8:6). As we will see, God also used word pictures and other symbols to communicate a truth to one group of people while hiding it from others who were not willing to believe (Mark 4:11, 4:33). All such symbols were significant, however, and no superfluous information was ever given to

cloud the truth God wanted to communicate. By far, the majority of what God wanted to communicate to all mankind for all time was communicated by spoken or written word, or was clearly explained as the correct interpretation of a vision. The children of Israel were instructed to pass on God's truths to their children by the spoken word (Exod. 10:2; Ps. 78:1-8) and the written word (Deut. 6:9, 11:20, 27:2-8).

Take careful note of the following verses, which all emphasize the Word of God as the single vehicle for communicating God's complete truth to man in all ages:

> Thy word have I hid in mine heart, that I might not sin against thee.
> —Psalms 119:11

> Through thy precepts I get understanding: therefore I hate every false way.
> —Psalms 119:104

> Thy word is a lamp unto my feet, and a light unto my path.
> —Psalms 119:105

The entrance of thy words giveth light; it giveth understanding unto the simple. (Even the simple can be enlightened by God's Word. This word for simple in the Greek can mean naive or open minded, both describing a child. Compare with Mark 10:15.)
—Psalms 119:130

Order my steps in thy word: and let not any iniquity have dominion over me.
—Psalms 119:133

Thy word is very pure: therefore thy servant loveth it.
—Psalms 119:140

Sanctify them through thy truth: thy word is truth.
—John 17:17

So then faith cometh by hearing, and hearing by the Word of God. (Also compare this with 1 Cor. 1:21 on preaching the spoken word.)
—Romans 10:17

So that thou incline thine ear unto wisdom, and apply thine heart to understanding.
—Proverbs 2:2

> For the LORD giveth wisdom: out of his mouth cometh knowledge and understanding.
> —Proverbs 2:6

> Get wisdom, get understanding: forget it not; neither decline from the words of my mouth.
> —Proverbs 4:5

> I will worship toward thy holy temple, and praise thy name for thy lovingkindness and for thy truth: for thou hast magnified thy word above all thy name.
> —Psalms 138:2

The name of God is indeed awesome and great, but in Psalm 138:2 He says He has magnified His Word even above His name, giving the highest importance to His written and spoken word (also see Ps. 138:4). Matthew 4:4 says "It is written, man shall not live by bread alone, but by every word that proceedeth out of the mouth of God" (also see Deut. 8:3).

Chapter 4

# Pictures in Scripture

**G**OD USED PICTORIAL methods in Scripture. The pictures included metaphoric word pictures, parables, abstract dreams (visions) and physical object lessons in which the observer actually took part. None of these pictorial methods left anything to the imagination of the observer or conveyed anything superfluous to the exact facts intended. While some might argue that not all parables were explained, and that they are left to the imagination of the observer, I would argue that either the meaning of the parable was deliberately hidden until such time as its meaning will become apparent, or, that the parable was understood perfectly by those to whom it was given, even if we do not understand it today.

## 1. Metaphoric Word Pictures

When one object or person is used to describe and convey deeper meaning about another object or person, this is called a metaphoric word picture. Some examples include the bread and cup representing the body and blood of Christ in Luke 22:19-20, the Lord describing Himself as the door in John 10:9, as the bread of life in John 6:35 and 6:48-51, as the light of the world in John 8:12, as the good shepherd in John 10:11-14, and as the true vine John 15:1.

Other examples of metaphoric word pictures include the ark of Noah being used as a figure of baptism in Christ (1 Pet. 3:20), the example of spiritual armour (Eph. 6:13-17), the church representing the body of Christ (1 Cor. 12:27), and our physical bodies depicting the temple of the Holy Spirit (1 Cor. 6:19-20). Olive plants are likened to children, and a wife a fruitful vine in Psalm

128:3. Trees are also used to demonstrate strength of character and integrity in Judges 9:8-21 and 2 Kings 14:9.

## 2. Parables

A parable is a story used to teach a truth. In all parables, the characters and other objects are all necessary in order to comprehend the meaning of the story. None is superfluous. A parable usually had two audiences, one to which the meaning was made known, and another to which the meaning was hidden. The attitude of the heart determined which audience the hearer belonged to (Mark 4:11). The interpretation of the parable was specifically defined, that is, it was not left to the hearer to decide on its meaning or application.

Here are some examples of parables from the gospel of Matthew:

The Sower (13:1-18)
The Wheat and the Tares (13:24-30, 13:36-43)
The Grain of Mustard Seed (13:31-32)

The Leaven (13:33)
The Treasure (13:44)
The Pearl (13:45-46)
The Net (13:47-50)
The Vineyard (21:33-44)
The Marriage (22:1-13)
The Fig Tree (24:32-33)

## 3. Visions

God communicated visions in dreams either through abstract concepts requiring an interpretation by another messenger of God (2 Chron. 6:5, Dan. 1:17), or in plain speech readily understood by the one to whom the vision was given (Num. 12:6). The one to whom the vision was given may have been awake (Num. 24:4) or asleep (Gen. 15:12-21). Examples of visions in the Bible include:

Abraham (Gen. 15:1)
Abimilech (Gen. 20:3)
Jacob/Israel (Gen. 31:11, 46:2)
Laban (Gen. 31:24)
Joseph (Gen. 37:5-10)

Butler and Baker, interpreted by Joseph (Gen. 40:5-14)
Pharoah (Gen. 41:1-32)
Gideon's Enemies (Judges 7:13-15)
Samuel (1 Sam. 3:11-15)
Nathan (2 Sam. 7:4-17)
Solomon (1 Kings 3:5-15)
Isaiah (Isa. 1)
Ezekiel (Ezek. 1)
Nebuchadnezzar (Dan. 2:3-45, 4:5-24)
Daniel (Dan. 2:19, 7-12)
Peter (Acts 10:9-29)
John (Revelation)

## 4. Object Lessons

An object lesson was a real life lesson in which the participant was required to do certain things in order to learn what God was trying to teach him or what God wanted him to teach others. This was usually a very tangible lesson where the participant felt the emotions and the deep anguish or joy of the lessons being taught in such a vivid way that he was able to communicate this truth with zeal and conviction.

Some examples of these life pictures include Ezekiel (Ezek. 4-5), Hosea (Hosea 1-3) and Paul (Acts 21:11). Since metaphoric word pictures and parables are really both cases of the written or spoken word, visions and object lessons are the only other pictorial methods used in Scripture. When God used such pictorial methods, there was never room for misinterpretation or the conveying of unnecessary or misleading information. Such object lessons were generally given to provide messengers with the tangible experience necessary to speak with the boldness, conviction and urgency intended by God. Thus, object lessons were a vehicle for enhancing the presentation of the spoken or written word.

If a picture in Scripture is unclear to the reader today, it is either because the reader is not yet enlightened, still having more study to immerse himself in, or has the wrong heart attitude and thus can't receive the meaning, or because God has hidden the meaning until such time as it is relevant. One thing we can be certain of: God reveals to us exactly what we need to know when we need to know it, provided one is regenerated and thus has the Holy Spirit as teacher. If one diligently and studiously seeks the Lord's will to know God's heart through His revealed Word, Scripture promises that the Holy Spirit will enlighten and reward that person's search.

Isaiah 48:8-10 says, "Remember this, and shew yourselves men: bring it again to mind, O ye transgressors. Remember the former things of old: for I am God, and there is none else; I am God, and there is none like me. Declaring the end from the beginning, and from ancient times the things that are not yet done, saying, My counsel shall stand, and I will do all my pleasure." The writer of Hebrews says that "without faith it is impossible to please him: for he that cometh to God must believe that he is, and that he is a rewarder of them that diligently seek him" (11:6).

What is faith? Hebrews 11:1 says, "Now faith is the substance of things hoped for, the evidence of things not seen." How is one to find understanding and the knowledge of God? "Yea, if thou criest after knowledge, and liftest up thy voice for understanding; if thou seekest her as silver, and searchest for her as for hid treasures; then shalt thou understand the fear of the LORD, and find the knowledge of God. (Prov. 2:3-4). Psalms 25:14 says "the secret of the LORD is with them that fear him; and he will shew them his covenant." Proverbs 1:5-6 teaches that "a wise man will hear, and will increase learning; and a man of understanding shall attain unto wise counsels. To understand a proverb, and the interpretation; the words of the wise, and their dark sayings."

Also see Job 24:1; Proverbs 2:6-7, 2:10-12, 9:10, 18:1; Isaiah 48:5-7; Daniel 2:20-23, 12:4-13; John 4:25, 15:15, 16:30, 21:17; and Acts 1:7.

## Chapter 5

# Images Lead to Destruction

AN IMAGE IS either a drawing or statue of a created being, or an object representing something which is then exalted in one's mind, taking the place of the original being. The key to the problem is "taking the place." When one recalls the original being, the substitute is what is remembered, admired, and even worshiped. The image is our creation and not God's, putting our creation in place of God's creation and robbing Him of His glory. "Isn't that picture of a bear cute?" instead of "Isn't the bear God made fierce and powerful?" Isaiah 42:8 records God saying, "I am the LORD: that is my name: and my glory will I not give to another, neither my praise to graven images."

Let us consider some verses describing images leading us astray:

> Thou shalt not make unto thee any graven image, or any likeness of any thing that is in heaven above, or that is in the earth beneath, or that is in the water under the earth.
> —Exodus 20:4

One might argue that the context goes on to indicate the bowing down to or worshiping of the image which is the forbidden thing rather than the image itself. This may be so, but the number of times the very image itself caused people to go astray from the truth is indicative of the underlying issue of the dependence on images. As Isaiah 42:8 also describes, man gives the attention and praise to the image rather than to God. The very indignation against the thrust of this book is in itself an indication of the status we give images and is a form of idolatry, being unable to communicate without them.

Genesis 31:19-35 tells the story of Rachel stealing, and then lying about, the images representing her father's false gods.

Exodus 32:22-25 tells the story of the children of Israel asking Aaron to make them a golden calf to represent the god who brought them out of Egypt. It wasn't good enough for them to worship an invisible God, especially when His representative, Moses, had apparently disappeared. How could any golden god part the waters of the Red Sea? Give them water from a rock? Feed them manna? Guide them in their physical journey? Ensure that their clothes and footwear didn't wear out? Yet they wanted a god of gold instead. This image, or substitute, robbed God of His rightful glory and could not be compared in any way with the true God and His numerous attributes and glories.

> Ye shall make you no idols nor graven image, neither rear you up a standing image, neither shall ye set up any image of stone in your land, to bow down unto it: for I am the LORD your God.
> —Leviticus 26:1

Then ye shall drive out all the inhabitants of the land from before you, and destroy all their pictures, and destroy all their molten images, and quite pluck down all their high places.

—Numbers 33:52

Take ye therefore good heed unto yourselves; for ye saw no manner of similitude on the day that the LORD spake unto you in Horeb out of the midst of the fire: Lest ye corrupt yourselves, and make you a graven image, the similitude of any figure, the likeness of male or female, the likeness of any beast that is on the earth, the likeness of any winged fowl that flieth in the air, the likeness of any thing that creepeth on the ground, the likeness of any fish that is in the waters beneath the earth. And lest thou lift up thine eyes unto heaven, and when thou seest the sun, and the moon, and the stars, even all the host of heaven, shouldest be driven to worship them, and serve them, which the LORD thy God hath divided unto all nations under the whole heaven.

—Deuteronomy 4:15-19

Take heed unto yourselves, lest ye forget the covenant of the LORD your God, which he made with you, and make you a graven image, or the

likeness of any thing, which the LORD thy God hath forbidden thee.
—Deuteronomy 4:23

Thou shalt not make thee any graven image, or any likeness of any thing that is in heaven above, or that is in the earth beneath, or that is in the waters beneath the earth.
—Deuteronomy 5:8

Neither shalt thou set thee up any image; which the LORD thy God hateth.
—Deuteronomy 16:22

Cursed be the man that maketh any graven or molten image, an abomination unto the LORD, the work of the hands of the craftsman, and putteth it in a secret place. And all the people shall answer and say, Amen.
—Deuteronomy 27:15

Judges 8:24-27 tells us about Gideon causing Israel to go astray by creating a golden image which the people then worshiped.

Judges 17-18 tells the story of Micah who set up an idol and false priesthood and ensnared the tribe of Dan until the captivity.

> And there they left their images, and David and his men burned them.
> —2 Samuel 5:21

> And they left all the commandments of the LORD their God, and made them molten images, even two calves, and made a grove, and worshiped all the host of heaven, and served Baal.
> —2 Kings 17:16

> He removed the high places, and brake the images, and cut down the groves, and brake in pieces the brazen serpent that Moses had made: for unto those days the children of Israel did burn incense to it: and he called it Nehushtan.
> —2 Kings 18:4

2 Kings 23 tells us the story of Josiah, who ridded the land of images and idolatry.

> Every man is brutish in his knowledge: every founder is confounded by the graven image: for his molten image is falsehood, and there is no breath in them.
> —Jeremiah 10:14

Daniel 3 tells us the story of the great image worshiped at the sound of the music.

What profiteth the graven image that the maker thereof hath graven it; the molten image, and a teacher of lies, that the maker of his work trusteth therein, to make dumb idols?
—Habakkuk 2:18

And when the townclerk had appeased the people, he said, Ye men of Ephesus, what man is there that knoweth not how that the city of the Ephesians is a worshipper of the great goddess Diana, and of the image which fell down from Jupiter?
—Acts 19:35

Because that, when they knew God, they glorified him not as God, neither were thankful; but became vain in their imaginations, and their foolish heart was darkened. Professing themselves to be wise, they became fools, and changed the glory of the uncorruptible God into an image made like to corruptible man, and to birds, and fourfooted beasts, and creeping things.
—Romans 1:21-23

Before you throw your hands up in despair and conclude that all of these verses are irrelevant, consider carefully the connection between the image and the distraction leading to false worship and destruction. The very reason images are forbidden is because of man's reliance on them rather than God and His Word. Take note again of Numbers 33:52, "Then ye shall drive out all the inhabitants of the land from before you, and destroy all their pictures, and destroy all their molten images, and quite pluck down all their high places." The prophet Habakkuk describes an image as "a teacher of lies" (2:18).

The Lord also warned us about the eye and how it can fill the body with light or darkness, and this is not just physical but spiritual light and darkness. That is, what we allow ourselves to see may cause spiritual enlightenment or spiritual blindness. Luke 11:34 says "the light of the body is the eye: therefore when thine eye is single, thy whole body also is full of light; but when thine eye is evil, thy body also is full of darkness."

We are not to be dependent on the physical senses to impart direction, but rather on faith alone. In 2 Corinthians 5:7 the apostle Paul says, "For we walk by faith, not by sight," and in Romans 1:17 he says, "The just shall live by faith."

The pattern in Scripture to teach truth is through the written or spoken word. The overwhelming majority of passages dealing with pictures and images paints them in a very negative light, because people become dependent on them and because their focus is on the image rather than what it represents. Pictures and images simply become a feast for the lust of the eyes (1 John 2:16; Ecc. 1:8). If Scripture alone is our guide to the correct method to impart wisdom and knowledge, then the method we should use is the written and spoken word without images or pictures, especially images or pictures which contradict the text itself. David's resolve to set no wicked thing before his eyes (Ps. 101:3) should be our resolve as well. The Word of God alone applied to the heart brings wisdom, understanding, and ultimately salvation.

*Chapter 6*

# Thinking Like a Child

**T**HINKING LIKE A child is not something an adult can do by thinking how a child would think. It is thinking how a child thinks. God created children to receive simple truths. There is no need to distort them or hide them amongst the confusion of non-essential images so that the child is always forced to distinguish fact from the fiction. Why cloud the message? Why make the story "cute" by adding distractions? Remember why God would not allow images to be drawn or carved. It was because it was so easy for them to be worshiped and, as already noted, images lead to distraction from the truth.

Paul describes the progression from thinking like a child to thinking like an adult as simply moving from a simple understanding to a fuller one, not from silliness to sensibility. Here is how he put it in 1 Corinthians 13:11-12: "When I was a child, I spake as a child, I understood as a child, I thought as a child: but when I became a man, I put away childish things. For now we see through a glass, darkly; but then face to face: now I know in part; but then shall I know even as also I am known."

Matthew's gospel says "And Jesus called a little child unto him, and set him in the midst of them, and said, 'Verily I say unto you, except ye be converted, and become as little children, ye shall not enter into the kingdom of heaven. Whosoever therefore shall humble himself as this little child, the same is greatest in the kingdom of heaven.'" (18:2-4). And Mark's gospel shares the same thought: "Verily I say unto you, Whosoever shall not receive the kingdom of God as a little child, he shall not enter therein" (10:15).

Compare what an adult writes about how a child thinks to the writings of a child who has not been tainted with so-called children's stories by adult authors. Adults tend to think that children love fantasy and make believe. Actually, children love truth. They may have a simple understanding of that truth, but they love truth. Having six children of my own so far, I know that the overwhelming majority of questions children ask are about the true world where they live, not the fantasy world created by adults for children. It is adults who taint the minds of children by creating fantasy. Children may pretend, but pretending or playing games about reality is different from the fantasy created in the minds of adult authors for children.

If we look to Scripture alone, we find that children did not spend endless hours in a fantasy world created by adults. Since Scripture alone should be our model, it should be our guide on what to expect from our children at various ages, how they think, and what level of understanding is reasonable for them.

Samuel was serving the Lord under the instruction of Eli from the time he was weaned (1 Sam. 1:22-28, 2:11, 2:18-19, 3:1-10). He was capable of remembering and relaying God's message for Eli accurately, even at this young age (1 Sam. 3:15-18). Naaman's wife had a servant girl who was responsible and knowledgeable enough and had faith in the God of Israel to recommend her master seek healing from Elisha (2 Kings 5:1-8). Other children we find in the Bible are Josiah, who was eight years old (2 Kings 22:1), and Joash, who was seven (2 Chron. 24:1) when they began their reign as kings. Timothy learned the Scriptures as a child (2 Tim. 3:15). The Lord Jesus was about His Heavenly Father's business, taking care of himself and interacting intelligently with the teachers of the law at the age of twelve (Luke 2:42-49).

Nor were children separated from their parents during times of public teaching and worship (Deut. 29:10-12, 31:12; Josh. 8:35; 2 Chron. 20:13; Ezra 10:1; Neh. 8:1-3; and Matt. 14:21, 15:38.) The modern idea that children should be in Sunday schools or age-segregated activities is foreign to the Scriptures, and this is why children during Biblical times were able to understand and accomplish much more at a younger age.

The Lord Jesus tells us in Matthew 8:2 that a little child can enter into the kingdom of heaven (or can understand the truths enabling him or her to be a subject of the King of the heavens). In their simplicity and humility of mind, as yet untainted by theories and philosophies, they can grasp the plain truths of the Word of God. If we as adults do not receive the truths with the humility and simplicity of a child, we will not be able to enter the kingdom of heaven. It is the complication of the simple Word of God by our vain philosophies that prevent us from having the clear minded and unadulterated child-like faith necessary to enter heaven. Thus, as adults, thinking like a child in order to write so-called children's books is actually quite difficult because of our accumulated baggage.

What we learn then from Scripture confirms Paul's statement that childishness is not silliness but instead a simple understanding that becomes mature thought through training, until the time it becomes wisdom. He said "now I know in part; but then shall I know even as also I am known" (1 Cor. 13:12). The revelation of God's

Word brings light and understanding, even to children (Ps. 119:130). Children have a simple, uncomplicated and unadulterated understanding of things, and ultimately it is God's Word alone that brings light to the child's simple mind.

## Chapter 7

# Why Read?

SOLOMON'S WORDS TO his son were key instruction for me growing up. "And further, by these, my son, be admonished: of making many books there is no end; and much study is a weariness of the flesh. Let us hear the conclusion of the whole matter: Fear God, and keep his commandments: for this is the whole duty of man" (Eccles. 12:12-13).

It is thus with care that I add yet another book to the load which causes the soul to be wearied and yet the admonition has a conclusion which is the goal of this short appeal. The purpose of reading is to equip the reader to fear God and keep His commandments. That is, to draw his attention back to his awe inspiring and worship desiring Creator. It is to cause him to be silent before the true God whose character and works should fill every sense given him by God, to bring him into the place of total and utter dependence upon and submission to Him.

Reading should not be time filler, entertainment, lust gratification or a stumbling block to idolatry. Knowledge for knowledge's sake puffeth up (1 Cor. 8:1), yet knowledge mixed with wisdom is a gem worthy of our diligent and deliberate desire and search (2 Chron. 1:10-12; Prov. 1:7, 2:6, 2:10, 8:12, 9:10, 24:13-14; Eccles. 2:26, 7:12; Isa. 33:6; Dan. 1:4, 2:21; Eph. 1:17; Col 1:9; and James 3:13).

If knowledge mixed with wisdom is the goal for believers, it should also be the goal of believers for their children. Thus, any book we lay before the eyes of our precious blessings should result in bringing that young soul into a love relationship of total dependence and faith in our Creator and Saviour.

Unless we renew our minds, we cannot attain knowledge and wisdom and know the perfect will of God for our lives. Renewing is the process of identifying and ridding our thinking of every vain philosophy exalting itself against God. This leads to having the mind of Christ. "Let this mind be in you, which was also in Christ Jesus" (Phil. 2:5). The apostle Paul wrote "And be not conformed to this world: but be ye transformed by the renewing of your mind, that ye may prove what is that good, and acceptable, and perfect, will of God" (Rom. 12:2). He also spoke of "Casting down imaginations, and every high thing that exalteth itself against the knowledge of God, and bringing into captivity every thought to the obedience of Christ" (2 Cor. 10:5).

When we read a Christian book, we should come away with the truth. We need to be careful we don't read the truth but remember a lie, or read the truth but remember nothing of any significance. A Christian book—what is that? Is it possible to divorce Christ from our knowledge? I think not. For it is Christ who gives that knowledge. There should be no division of secular and sacred. As Christians, bearing the name of Christ, being in the world and yet not of it, every fact taught to our children must be taught in the context of the God who gave that fact—in other words, a biblical worldview. For there is nothing in the entire universe, not anything that has been discovered or manufactured, that God did not first create.

*Chapter 8*

# Excuses

LET US EXAMINE some of the excuses for using cartoons to teach truth.

*Children need pictures to reinforce the words in books.* No, this is false. We adults make our children dependent upon them. What was life like before the color printer? God's method for imparting truth has nothing to do with pictures.

*We need pictures to instill creativity in our children.* No, this is not true, either. God created us in His own image. He is the Creator and we are provided with His characteristics, and this includes (in a much lesser sense) creativity.

*Imagination is good, and children need pictures to inflate the imagination.* No, they don't. Creativity is good, being able to think beyond the here and now is good, but fantasy is dwelling on lies. We are told to think on whatsoever is true and whatsoever is honest (Phil. 4:8). Children do not need to be taught lies.

*Our parents taught us that way and their parents before them, and we're OK.* Nehemiah 8:14-17 describes the recovering of truth not taught since the days of Joshua, the son of Nun, and this was hundreds of years. Josiah also recovered the truth lost for many years (2 Kings 22:8-13). The point is that time is no excuse for continuing the pattern of sin or bad practice. Using this reasoning, we'd never repent.

*All the verses in the Bible against the use of images were directed to the Jews and not to us.* This needs to be clarified. Remember that the Jews were supposed to be a light to the nations, demonstrating the goodness and sensibility of God's precepts (Deut. 4:5-9). Paul told us that "All scripture is given by inspiration of God, and is profitable for doctrine, for reproof, for correction, for instruction in righteousness: That the man of God may be perfect, throughly furnished unto all good works" (2 Tim. 3:16-17). The valuable and practical instruction given to the Jews in their law is not to be discarded just because we cannot obtain salvation through keeping the law (Gal 2:16, 3:11). As students of God's Word we must glean the principles and practical truths from this instruction (1 Cor 10:1-12). We must receive wisdom from the lessons that they learned in order not to make the same mistakes which they made.

# Conclusion

**T**HIS PRESENT DISCUSSION of images is in the context of children's books. The scriptural backing is quoted to demonstrate the connection between images and the going astray of the observer, and it is not meant to eliminate the judicial and wise use of accurate drawings or real life photos from our lives. It is fitting, however, to remember that a photo is a snapshot of a single instance in time and may not even represent the most important or realistic snapshot of that event, but it is what is remembered. How often have we felt intimidated by that perfect portrait of another family appearing to have it "all together" as we consider the average day of trials in our own imperfect family? This discussion is meant to expose the prevalence of erroneous images in children's media and highlight the danger of dualism and its result: the destruction of our children's scriptural foundation before it is even completed. It is to demonstrate the superiority of the tried and true method of imparting knowledge and wisdom to our children, the method God ordained and used throughout history, that of the written and spoken word alone.

If we must use pictures in our books, the pictures we use should be very carefully chosen such that they in no way undermine, detract or wrongly emphasize something clearly described and adequately explained by the words themselves. Before using pictures, we need to decide what the facts are, and where the focus is. Unhelpful pictures amount to information overload and a watering down of or blatant denial of the truth. Is the focus of the picture confirming or undermining the words of Scripture? Is the picture emphasizing something the words give little emphasis to, or detracting from something the words speak volumes about? Will the picture be remembered instead of what it represents? Worse still, will it be worshiped instead of God? Does the picture rob God of His rightful glory?

If a picture paints a thousand words, then let those thousand words be a thousand words of truth, for if just ten words be errant then we have perpetrated a lie and injected the recipe of rat poison (ninety-nine percent good and one percent death) into the heart and soul of our children. This mixture is enough to destroy a child's grasp of the total truth intended by the picture. In truth however, many children's books are much worse than this concoction, containing ninety percent lies with only ten percent or less truth. How much more destructive do you suppose that is?

We must never forget the Lord Jesus' warning. "Then said he unto the disciples, it is impossible but that offences will come: but woe unto him, through whom they come! It were better for him that a millstone were hanged about his neck, and he cast into the sea, than that he should offend one of these little ones" (Luke 17:1-2).

Is it possible to learn without picture books? It is indeed possible, and I can say this unequivocally as I was born blind! While we live in a world of imagery, if the imagery undermines the truth then we are better off without it—or even our eyes for that matter (Matt. 5:29). If the Bible is our standard for all matters of faith and practice, it should dictate how we impart truth to our children to ensure we give them a firm foundation on which the wise man can build a house that will endure any storm, no matter how vehement.

www.ingramcontent.com/pod-product-compliance
Lightning Source LLC
Chambersburg PA
CBHW031428290426
44110CB00011B/574